Dögs

Big and small	2
Different dogs	4
The dog family	6
Working dogs	8
My dog	10
Story: The Big Show	11
Activities	25
Picture Dictionary	30

Written by Paul Shipton

Illustrated by Andy Hammond and Red Giraffe

Big and small

There are 200 million pet dogs around the world. Dogs can be different shapes and sizes. This dog is very tall. It is called an Irish Wolfhound. It can be 86 centimetres tall.

This dog is big and strong, but it can be very friendly.

Some small dogs are called toy dogs. This small dog is from Mexico. It is only 15 centimetres tall.

This dog has got big eyes and big ears.

One Yorkshire Terrier in England was only 6.3 centimetres tall and 9.5 centimetres long.

Different dogs

There are many different kinds of dogs. Some dogs haven't got any hair. Some dogs have got long, straight hair.

This dog has got curly, black hair.

This dog is very old. It was a pet in Egypt a long time ago.

Some dogs can run very fast. This dog is a Greyhound. It has got long legs, a thin face and small ears.

World Record!

Greyhound runs at over 67 kilometres an hour.

Australia, 1994

This dog runs in races.

The dog family

All dogs eat meat. Wolves and foxes are in the dog family. In Britain, foxes sometimes live in towns and cities. The Arctic Wolf has got white fur in the winter.

This fox has got red fur and a thick tail.

This Arctic Wolf has got sharp teeth, thick fur and strong legs.

This dog is called a dingo. It lives in Australia. Dingoes are not pets. They are wild dogs.

This dingo has got brown fur.

Jackals are in the dog family, but hyenas are not.

Jackal

Hyena

Working dogs

Not all dogs are pets. Some dogs work. People can train dogs to do lots of clever things.

The owner of this dog can't see. The dog is her 'eyes'. This dog is called a guide dog.

This dog works with sheep. It listens to the farmer's whistle.

This dog is a German Shepherd. They are strong and clever. They are one of the most useful dogs in the world.

This dog is a German Shepherd. They are strong and clever. They are one of the most useful dogs in the world.

The Big Show

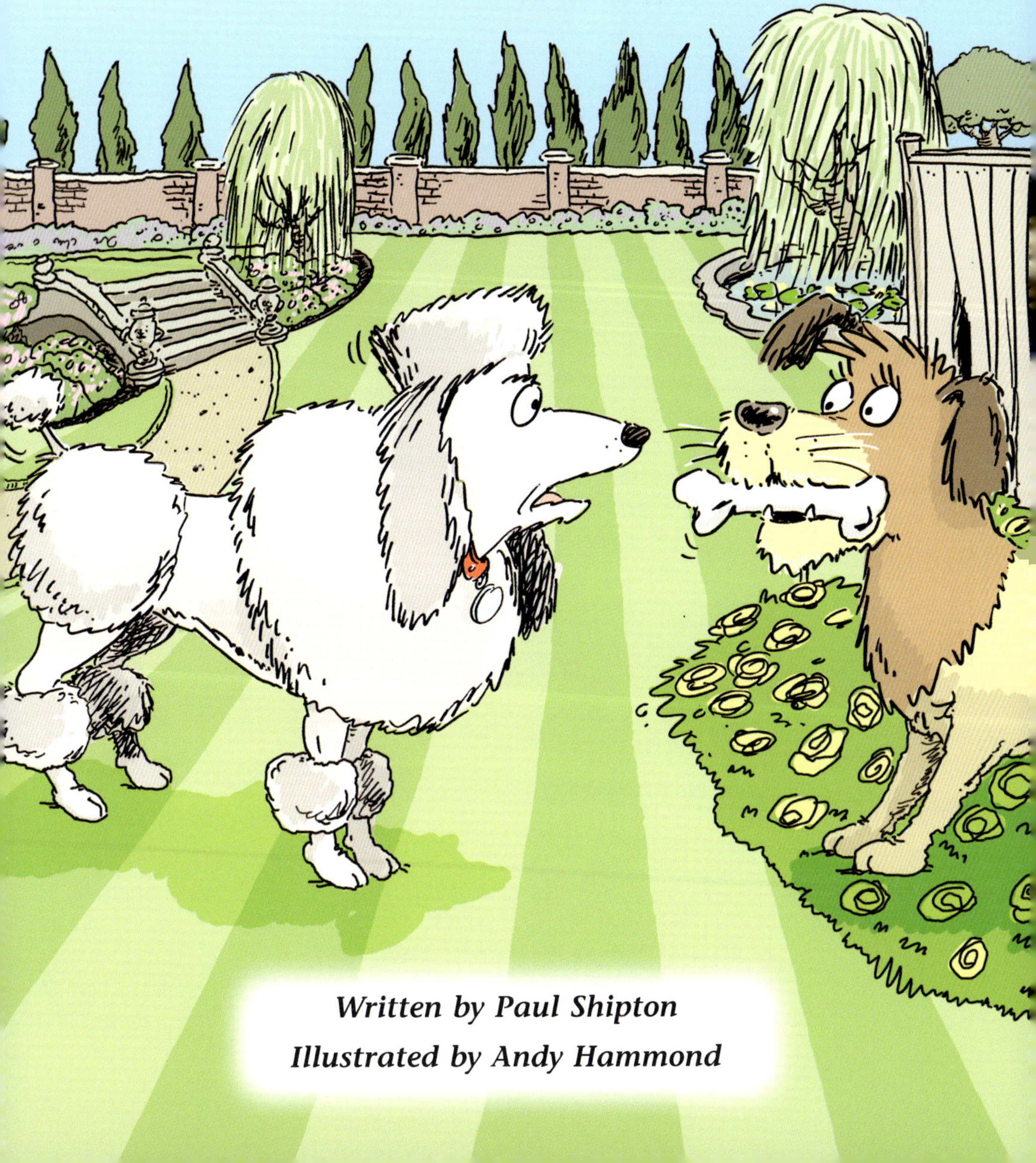

Written by Paul Shipton

Illustrated by Andy Hammond

Percy is a white dog. He lives in a big house. He eats nice food. But today he isn't happy.

Suddenly, there's another dog in the garden – a very different dog. She hasn't got an owner or a big house. She lives in the streets.

Ella runs into the pet carrier and Percy runs off with the bone.

Percy is happy. But there is a big dog in the street. He's very angry. He wants Percy's bone. Percy is afraid. He runs away.

This is Percy's owner. She is called Mrs Plumley.

Ella doesn't want to go to the dog show. But she is in the taxi. She can't escape.

Ella is at the dog show. She is looking at three other dogs. They have got lots of questions for her.

Here is Mrs Plumley. She can't see Percy. She sees Ella, instead!

The door is open. Ella runs away!

Percy is in the street. He isn't happy.

Inside, Ella is hiding in a dark room with lots of gold trophies. She sees two robbers come in.

Ella runs after the two robbers. She barks at them. Soon all the other dogs are barking, too.

The robbers run to the door. But here's Percy! His nice fur is wet and dirty. He's very angry. The robbers are afraid.

The police take the robbers away. Percy is happy. Mrs Plumley is happy …

… and Ella is happy, too.

Activities

1 Look and write.

eyes ears face legs ~~tail~~ teeth hair feet

2 Match the sentences to the pictures.

He is sleeping. [2]

She is barking. [ ]

He is jumping. [ ]

She is eating. [ ]

He is drinking. [ ]

She is running. [ ]

3 **Look at the pictures and read the sentences. Write A or B.**

A

B

1 This dog has got long hair. B

2 This dog has got a thin face.

3 This dog has got a short tail.

4 This dog has got long legs and short hair.

5 This dog is small.

4 **Look and write.**

This dog has got ______________________

____

______________________.

5 Match the sentences.

1 Sky eats	water.
2 She plays	in a basket.
3 She drinks	good food.
4 She has two long	walks every day.
5 She sleeps	with a ball.

6 Circle T (True) or F (False).

1	Ella lives in a big house.	T F
2	Percy's owner is called Mrs Plumley.	T F
3	Ella goes to the dog show.	T F
4	Ella wants to go to the dog show.	T F
5	Ella runs after the robbers.	T F
6	The robbers are not afraid of Percy.	T F
7	The robbers escape.	T F

7 Who says it? Match the sentences to the pictures.

1 I want to live in a big house and eat nice food.

2 Give me your bone!

3 Who is that terrible, dirty dog?

4 I want to be free.

5 Quick! Put them in the bag!

8 Complete the sentences.

dirty	escapes	~~happy~~	open	want	wet

1 Fritz is not __happy__ . He does not ________ to have a bath. He does not want to get ________.

2 The window is ________. Fritz runs to it and ________.

3 Now Fritz is wet and ________!

Picture Dictionary

world

wolf

fox

sheep

farmer

jackal

hyena

dingo

leg

face

ears

eyes

tail

teeth

whistle

police

food

garden

street

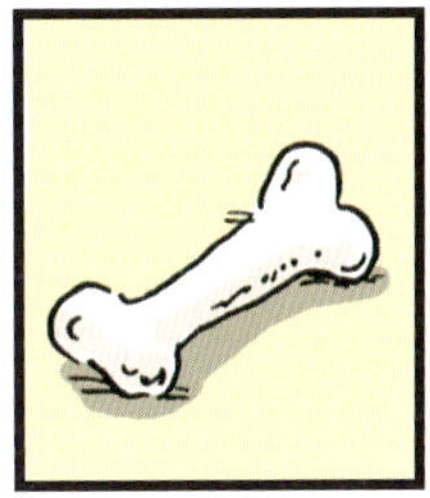
bone

pet carrier

door

robber

trophy

bag

run

bark

dirty

happy

wet

afraid

angry

Macmillan Education
4 Crinan Street
London N1 9XW
A division of Springer Nature Limited
Companies and representatives throughout the world

ISBN 978-1-3800-3772-5
ISBN 978-1-3800-3771-8 (International Edition)

First published 2007
This edition published 2019

Designed by Red Giraffe Limited
Illustrated by Andy Hammond and Red Giraffe Limited

The author and publishers would like to thank the following for permission to reproduce their photographs:

Cover Photography with the kind permission of Ardea/John Daniels

Ardea/Ian Beames (LBO) p6(t), Ardea/Jean-Michel Labat p8(t); Corbis/Bojan Brecelj p4(b), Corbis/Tom Nebbia; FLPA/Mark Raycroft/ Minden Pictures pp1, 4(t), FLPA/David Dalton p3, FLPA/Jim Brandenburg/ Minden Pictures p6(b), FLPA/Martin B. Withers p7rt, Getty Images p8 (b); Getty Images/Robert Daly p2; Oxford Scientific Film/Charles Bowman p5, Photodisc p7(br), p7(l).

Printed and bound in Great Britain by Bell and Bain Ltd, Glasgow

2023 2022 2021 2020 2019
10 9 8 7 6 5 4 3 2